Slow Motion

The Log of a Chesapeake Bay Skipjack

by

M. Kei

Keibooks
Perryville, Maryland
2011

Slow Motion : The Log of a Chesapeake Bay Skipjack, Second Edition
Copyright 2011 by M. Kei. All rights reserved.

Front cover photograph, "*Martha Lewis* dredging for oysters" copyright 2005 by Amy Kehring (http://www.amy-kehring.com) and used with permission.

Back cover photograph of M. Kei aboard the Skipjack Martha Lewis credit Danna Cornick.

No part of this book may be reproduced in any form or by any means, except by a reviewer or scholar who may quote brief passages in a review or article.

ISBN 978-0615504872

Printed in the United States of America, 2011.

Keibooks
P O Box 516
Perryville, MD 21903
Keibooks@gmail.com

Poetry by M. Kei

Heron Sea, Short Poems of the Chesapeake Bay
Catzilla! : Tanka, Kyoka, and Gogyoshi about Cats (editor)
Fire Pearls : Short Masterpieces of the Human Heart (editor)
Atlas Poetica : A Journal of Poetry of Place in Contemporary Tanka (editor)
Take Five : Best Contemporary Tanka (editor-in-chief)

Fiction by M. Kei

Pirates of the Narrow Seas 1 : The Sallee Rovers
Pirates of the Narrow Seas 2 : Men of Honor
Pirates of the Narrow Seas 3 : Iron Men
Pirates of the Narrow Seas 4 : Heart of Oak

"There is nothing—absolutely nothing—half so much worth doing as simply messing about in boats."
~Kenneth Graham, The Wind in the Willows

Table of Contents

Introduction, 7

Havre de Grace to Deal Island, 15
1 September, 15
2 September, 25
3 September, 33
4 September, 41
5 September, 45

Interlude: The *Lantern Queen*, 53

Even Further South, 61
17 October, 61
18 October, 75
Red Cap Creek, 91
Crisfield Watermen's Festival, 97
20 October, 107
21 October, 121

Shore Leave: Making a Living on Land, 133

"Drudging Arsters," 137

Epilogue: Someone Else's Adventure, 149

Notes, 151

The Log of a Chesapeake Bay Skipjack

Introduction

The skipjack *Martha Lewis* is a workboat, one of the last vessels in North America to fish commercially under sail. Built as an oyster dredge by Bronza Parks of Wingate, Maryland, in 1955, she is one of the last of the historic skipjacks. In 1985, the Chesapeake Bay Skipjack Fleet was listed on the National Register of Historic Places, and in 2002, the fleet was named one of the "eleven most endangered places in America" by the National Historic Trust.

Skipjacks are unique in the world and developed in response to local conditions. Beginning in the early 1800s, the state of Maryland restricted methods for harvesting the oyster with the deliberate intention of conserving the abundant oyster beds of the Chesapeake Bay. Having seen the oyster beds of Long Island Sound and New England all but destroyed by steam-powered dredges, they wanted to sustain their harvest for future generations.

Oysters were therefore tonged by hand from small boats until the invention of the hand scrape in the 1840s. Hand tongs are a large set of tongs, something like salad tongs, but about ten to twenty feet long. They were (and still are) used from small boats in shallow waters, such as the log sailing canoe. Hand scrapes were a welcome invention. About the size of a modern lawn rake, they were dragged along the bottom to rake oysters into the attached bag. These small dredges were also illegal, but were winked at by the local authorities. Hand scrapes permitted watermen to harvest enough oysters not only to feed their families but to make a living bringing oysters to market. Oysters were an essential of the working class diet around the Bay because they were cheaper and more nutritious than chicken. In addition, live and canned oysters were shipped to the Midwest and Great Plains by trainload to be enjoyed by working people everywhere.

Eventually, in 1865, the illegal but successful experience with the hand scrapes persuaded the state of Maryland that the real culprit in oyster overharvesting was the steam engine, and so the dredge was legalized — but only under sail. That remained the law until 1966 when it was changed to permit the use of power two days a week. Thus watermen were guaranteed a catch even when the wind was unfavorable. Although 'environmentalism' and 'sustained harvest' sound very modern, in Maryland those efforts date back to the early 1800s and constitute one of the first efforts in the nation for the preservation and management of a natural resource.

The skipjack evolved to provide an economical, efficient, and stable platform for dredging. Technically a 'bateau', or shallow draft vessel used in protected waters, it is a 'boat' and not a 'ship'—a ship is a large vessel of three or more masts capable of traversing the ocean. The two-sail bateau acquired the nickname of 'skipjack' sometime in the early 1900s, perhaps because the way they skimmed along the water reminded the observer of the skipjack fish.

The skipjack has a simple design. With a bottom built principally from flat planks, it is characterized by a hard chine (a sharp turn where the sides turn under to form the bottom) as opposed to the round hull of a sloop. It could be built by a competent handyman from local timber. The few curved planks in the hull were not bent by steaming, but instead were 'plamfed' into position, a waterman's term which means getting every man in the boatyard to "push like a motherfucker." Brute force is often a sufficient and economical alternative to skill.

With a self-tending jib and a simple rig composed of one mast, two sails, and a minimum of lines, the skipjack could be handled in a pinch by a crew composed of a captain and deckhand. It isn't pleasant, but it can be done. (I have done it.) The mast is set well forward in the eyes of the boat, and the boom is so long it trails aft the transom. The mast is very tall, being built on a formula of "beam + length on deck = mast." A skipjack has a clipper bow and long sturdy bowsprit braced with chain shrouds, nicknamed 'whiskers.' Lazyjacks on the jib and mainsail catch the sails and prevent them from burying the deck when they are lowered. The jib lazyjacks are supported by a tringle, also called a 'spectacle fairline,' so named because on some vessels it looks like an old-fashioned pair of eyeglasses. 'Fairline' is one of those words that I have only heard and never seen written, so the spelling is debatable. It does not appear in any dictionary I have, not even Falconer's 1769 *Universal Dictionary of the Marine*, the mother-lode of archaic nautical terminology. Skipjack skills are traditional skills, learned by doing, not by reading.

The sails are a club-footed jib and a sharp-peaked, club-headed main, although very few skipjacks still retain their main club. The shrouds (lines to support the mast) and

Slow Motion

lazyjacks go to the hounds (a few feet below the top of the mast), and the mainsail is normally only raised to the hounds and not all the way to the mast top. Therefore, when dredging or racing, a club (a 6' long, 3-4" thick spar) is laced to the peak of the sail to needle it through the lazyjacks and so raise the great sail to its full height. The skipjack's main is probably the only club-headed sail in existence. This is so rare that seasoned sailors often correct me by saying, "You mean club-footed main." No, I don't.

The skipjack does have a club-footed jib. Yet with the normal wooden club in place it is difficult to make a skipjack sail wing and wing in light air (with the jib on one side and the mainsail on the other), therefore the wooden club is occasionally replaced with an extremely light plastic club, usually jury-rigged from scrap PVC pipe or other handy resource. With the waterman's economy of parlance, to sail wing and wing is to be 'wung out.' It permits the vessel to sail better when the wind is dead astern.

Compared to the more expensive round-hulled vessels with their greater manpower needs, a skipjack was inexpensive to build and to operate. Estimates vary wildly, but somewhere between 700 - 1000 were built. Their heyday was the late 1800s and early 1900s. Although they were economical at the time, times have since changed. It used to be that a man could go into his own woods and cut the timber he needed to build a skipjack, but since the virgin timber stands are gone, this is no longer possible. Traditionally, the local loblolly pines were used for the masts and booms, but when the *Martha Lewis* was restored during the winter of 1993-1994, no such timber could be found. Her mast and boom are now made from Douglas fir trucked in from Oregon. Thus the maintenance of such a vessel is extraordinarily expensive these days. When a captain-owner could no longer afford to maintain a skipjack, he left it in the marshes to die. Only a handful of captains are able to continue making a living by offering tourist cruises, a few are owned by non-profit organizations, and a handful have become playthings for the rich.

Because of the prohibition on engines for dredging, skipjacks have extremely large sails to develop the power necessary to pull the dredges. Each dredge weighs close to a hundred pounds empty. Full of oysters, mud and debris, they weigh several hundred pounds. In other words, they behave a lot like anchors. To power her dredges the *Martha Lewis* has 1942 square feet of sail, for which reason she keeps at least one reef tied in when not dredging or racing.

Innovative captains got around the law by using a 'pushboat' (also called a 'yawl boat') as a sort of miniature tugboat to push the skipjack out to the oyster beds and back to port. The pushboat is raised out of the water on davits while dredging. Department of Natural Resources (DNR) police inspect skipjacks at work to assure compliance with the law.

In 1966, in response to the decline of oysters on the Bay, the State of Maryland legalized the use of power two days a week so that the watermen were guaranteed a catch even in a week of no wind. Sadly, over-fishing, pollution, parasites, diseases, and development have continued to deplete the oyster stocks. Only 1-2% of the original oyster population remains. The consequence is a Chesapeake Bay full of greenish-brown murk, a murk which is accepted as

Slow Motion

normal by the Bay's inhabitants. But four hundred years ago when Captain John Smith (of Pocahontas fame) explored the Chesapeake Bay, he reported crystal clear water straight down to a sandy bottom. Oysters are filter feeders, meaning they suck in the water, consume whatever particles are in it, and spit out the water. Thus, whatever is carried in the water is ingested by the oyster, to its destruction. Mature oysters are not mobile, they cannot escape whatever is brought to them by the currents or a ship's wake.

The skipjack *Martha Lewis* was originally owned and operated by Captain Jim Lewis of Wingate, Maryland, on the Eastern Shore. Built by Bronza Parks in 1955, she is one of three sister boats whose keels were laid side by side on the grass and built together from the same plans. Her sisters are the *Rosie Parks* and the *Lady Katie,* each of which is undergoing restoration or repairs at this time. Bronza was murdered shortly after completing them; he had built a yacht for a man who disputed his asking price with a pistol. While most skipjacks "sailed like pigs," Bronza built his skipjacks to have better sailing qualities. His boats are not only stable work platforms, but fast sailers. *Martha's* top speed is 9 knots (about 10 mph). She is a frequent victor in skipjack races.

During the oyster heyday, Eastern Shore towns were as wild as any town of the 'Wild West,' and even now a bout of fisticuffs is not unknown among watermen. Watermen would even use their boats to fight. When oysters were profitable, watermen were in fierce competition to find and exploit oysters, and sometimes attempted to take them by force. When oysters began to decline, the competition became even sharper. With a long bowsprit and white hull, a skipjack is not unlike a medieval knight with his lance set, only much larger. Angry captains would charge each other, using their bowsprits as battering rams, swinging around to bump and smash like a demolition derby. Even in races dirty tricks are not unknown; a properly placed bowsprit can rip out the jib stays of an opposing vessel, thereby bringing down the mast. There is history in this, for the long sharp bow and bowsprit come from the Baltimore clipper, itself one of the myriad descendants of the Mediterranean war galley.

Skipjacks races are not the gentlemanly sport of yacht clubs; only in the most egregious cases will a foul be called. An opponent's bowsprit over your side all the way up to the winder box is not 'egregious.' On the other hand, as hard as they might compete, should a skipjack suffer genuine distress, all vessels will come to her aid. When a skipjack fails to return to port in severe weather, watermen do not wait for the Coast Guard but go out and attempt rescue themselves.

Characteristics that make *Martha* a fast boat also make her harder to steer, and so she is known to be the hardest to handle of the skipjacks. As Captain Bill, an experienced waterman, once told me, "You have to kick her ass before she kicks yours." Keeping a straight wake with her is constitutionally impossible, but Captain Bysshe, who was my first captain, could do it. He is an artist on the water. In normal operation *Martha* meanders along; the trick, as Captain Greg, her current captain says, is to nudge her zigzagging to coincide with the spaces between crab-pots and channel markers.

Slow Motion

Martha Lewis was saved by Dr. Randy George when she was about to be laid up, and she was restored over the winter of 1993 - 1994, the only year since her birth when she has not oystered. She is now owned and operated by a small, grassroots, non-profit organization with one and a half paid staff, the Chesapeake Heritage Conservancy. She continues oystering, as stipulated at the time of her restoration. The last time I oystered with *Martha*, we caught eight bushels of oysters, which brought $50 each. Six of us labored all day to get them. Traditionally, 30% of the catch went for the upkeep of the boat and the rest was split as shares among the crew. This explains why no one makes a living "drudging arsters" with a skipjack anymore. Those captains who still oyster do so on an occasional basis to keep their heritage alive. They are either retired or support themselves by doing other things.

I learned to sail on a skipjack. While I have occasionally given a hand on other historic vessels, I am proud to say I have never crewed on anything but wooden hulls. Thus I have learned my sailing the old-fashioned way, by learning from the men (and a few women), for whom 'wooden sail' is a way of life.

M. Kei
Perryville, Maryland
Chesapeake Bay, USA
11 November 2007

The Log of a Chesapeake Bay Skipjack

Havre de Grace to Deal Island, Or There and Back Again

September 1, 2007. 9 am, City Marina, Havre de Grace. Six crew, including the Captain, depart to carry the Skipjack Martha Lewis *over to Deal Island. The journey will take two days to get there, one to race, and two days to return.*

This is the 48th Deal Island Skipjack Race. Race sponsors searched for and found thirty-three skipjacks to whom they issued invitations. Ten accepted, nine showed up. The Nathan of Dorchester *was supposed to attend, but issues were discovered that bloomed into a major maintenance problem—a common complication with skipjacks. In the three years I have been crewing with the* Martha Lewis, *she has been through two such major overhauls. My first experience with* Martha *was caulking two-thirds of her starboard bottom and filling some two hundred nails holes in her port quarter.*

My children have also been pressed into service. My teenage daughter has painted the boot stripe on the pushboat, scraped paint from metal fittings, and marked boards. My teenage son has crawled through the bilge with me painting preservative and held the flashlight while I tarred the inside of the centerboard well. They drove down to Deal Island (school schedules not permitting them to make the full trip) and were aboard for the race.

Slow Motion

<u>September 1, Saturday, Labor Day weekend</u>

loading the boat . . .
pausing to watch
a bald eagle
carrying fish
to its nest

       Havre de Grace

ice chest
for a seat,
winder box
for my back,
sun on my chest

       off Havre de Grace

south of Spesutia Island,
a spider
reads over my shoulder

       off Spesutia Island

The Log of a Chesapeake Bay Skipjack

autumn morning—
cormorants winging past
faster than we can sail

off Spesutia Island

spray—
washed again by the wake
of a powerboat

off Spesutia Island

rounding Spesutia Island,
crab pots and
a crab boat working her line

off Spesutia Island

Slow Motion

passing the crab boat,
Aaramy, working a line
of black pennants

      off Spesutia Island

in the mouth
of the North East River,
lines of crab pots
and the low silhouettes
of crab boats at work

      off Spesutia Island

crossing our bow,
a squadron of
mute swans

      off Spesutia Island

The Log of a Chesapeake Bay Skipjack

coiling
the jib halyard,
I untangle a snarl,
'Men at Work'
on the satellite radio

    off Spesutia Island

working shirtless,
the sudden chill
of the mains'l's shadow

    off Spesutia Island

hat but
no shirt,
gloves but
no shoes —
summer sailing

    off Sassafras River

Slow Motion

Labor Day
on the Chesapeake Bay,
half the crew shirtless

        off Sassafras River

passing the
Sassafras River,
crab boats working
the lines,
pleasure boats under sail

        off Sassafras River

summer sandals,
tan lines on my feet

        off Sassafras River

The Log of a Chesapeake Bay Skipjack

coming up
on Worton Creek,
another flock
of sailboats
with white wings

off Worton Creek

the old lady
wants a new dress:
five patches
in her sail
and more needed

off Worton Creek

a convoy of trucks
crosses the Bay Bridge,
beneath them
an old skipjack
shakes out the last reef

Chesapeake Bay Bridge

Slow Motion

twin spans of
the Chesapeake Bay Bridge—
all that money spent,
you'd think at least
they'd match

Chesapeake Bay Bridge

the highest span
of the Bay Bridge,
a portapotty on
the work platform

Chesapeake Bay Bridge

Motor Vessel *Anna,*
her anchor as red
with rust
as the Russian star
on her bridge

Chesapeake Bay Bridge

The Log of a Chesapeake Bay Skipjack

we join a fleet of boats heading home—
but not ours

> *Severn River*

slowly
overtaking the schooner
with tanbark sails,
we join the sun
in Annapolis

> *Severn River*

following the sun
into golden Annapolis,
our workboat
not quite right for
'Ego Alley'

> *Severn River, Annapolis*

Slow Motion

Annapolis—
midis
in white uniforms,
buns neatly pinned up
under their hats

Annapolis harbor

The Log of a Chesapeake Bay Skipjack

Annapolis

The National Sailing Hall of Fame let us use their dock just outside of 'Ego Alley,' more properly known as Spa Creek, where million dollar yachts and cruise ships are docked. The scent of money clung to everything. Except us.

People gawked as our old wooden boat with her mended and stained sails came to rest alongside the pilings. To several perplexed people I replied, "It's a skipjack." A few of the tourists knew what they were looking at — you could tell by their air of suppressed excitement, like a birdwatcher spotting a rare endangered specie. As in truth the skipjack is.

We went to dinner at a rather nice restaurant along the waterfront: a pack of scruffy, tanned, bearded, stinky watermen. What a contrast with the crisp whites of the so very young midshipmen from the Naval Academy! The young men with their officer whites and short hair, the young women with their buns neatly tucked under their caps, all of them young enough to be our children and grandchildren.

Alas, we had arrived after the Harbormaster closed and had to cadge a single shower token from the janitor. The crew took showers in sequence, propping the door open for the guy behind us.

Slow Motion

September 2, Sunday

shoal waters
Thomas Point Lighthouse
splendid in the dawn

      off Severn River, Annapolis

the salt-streaked
roof of the Thomas Point
Lighthouse—
the age-stained sail
of a passing skipjack

      off Thomas Point Light

both sails set,
the mate at the helm,
the captain
takes a nap
in the mains'l's shade

      off Thomas Point Light

The Log of a Chesapeake Bay Skipjack

sails set
a deckhand
studies law

        off Thomas Point Light

sails set,
the oysterboat
heads south,
Thomas Point Light
shrinking in the distance

        off Thomas Point Light

dawn duties complete,
the sailors fill the morning
each according to his nature

        off Thomas Point Light

Slow Motion

the leaning tower
of Sharp's Island Light . . .
all that remains
of a vanished island,
a vanished time

   Sharp Island Shoals

Calvert Cliffs—
a schooner
the size of a moth

   off Calvert Cliffs

the chiming of
the bell buoy
ringing in the waves

   off Calvert Cliffs

The Log of a Chesapeake Bay Skipjack

a book for a pillow,
sleeping on
the swaying deck

> *off Calvert Cliffs*

broader still
the Chesapeake Bay,
each shore
the thinnest sketch
of line art

> *off Calvert Cliffs*

the slap of wind
the rumble of waves
the glittering sea

> *off Calvert Cliffs*

Slow Motion

again and again,
the snapping of the leech
against the topping lift

       off Hooper Island Light

passing a fish trap:
brown pelicans
black winged gulls
and ospreys
perched on the pilings

       off Hooper Island Light

seven brown pelicans
float unconcerned
about the great white bird
with men upon her back

       off Hooper Island Light

The Log of a Chesapeake Bay Skipjack

Deal Island night—
lazyjacks
full of stars

       Deal Island harbor

the night before the race,
halyards flapping
on the *City of Crisfield*

       Deal Island harbor

tall spars
full of stars . . .
can't sleep

       Deal Island harbor

Slow Motion

five days on a skipjack—
more Jimmy Buffet
than I can stand

> *Deal Island Harbor*

The Log of a Chesapeake Bay Skipjack

Deal Island

Deal Island is not the end of the world, but you can see it from there. The town of Chance—and 'town' is an exaggeration—still clings to the old harbor. I can't help but wonder if the original names were 'Last Chance' and 'Ordeal.' Coming into the harbor, skipjack masts could be seen rising above everything else. What a sight to see nine skipjacks in their natural habitat!

We rafted alongside the City of Crisfield, *an ancient skipjack that shows the toil of her years, to put it politely. I was careful where I put my feet crossing her deck for fear of plunging through a rotten spot.*

My son wanted to see the races, so my daughter drove him down in her pickup truck. She got a hotel because it was too late to drive back, but the closest one was twenty miles away in Princess Anne. My son slept on deck with me. It was cool, but the wind died down and we were warm enough under the harbor cover. Ashore the Jimmy Buffet tribute band kept banging away, heedless of the crews that would be rising at dawn to race.

Alas, our strategist missed the boat the next morning. As we were heading out to Tangier Sound, a motorboat raced to overtake us, Rick balancing on the bow. He leaped to our gunwale and climbed aboard like James Bond. Some people know how to make an entrance.

Slow Motion

<u>September 3, Labor Day Monday</u>

dawn
slept okay
warm enough,
only one spider
chummy with my pillow

   Deal Island harbor

Miss Ida May
accepts a seat on
our deck,
the skipjack *Ida May*
still being under repair

   Deal Island harbor

race day—
Tangier Sound
full of skipjacks
and pleasure boats

   Tangier Sound, off Deal Island

The Log of a Chesapeake Bay Skipjack

spending the night
with his woman, a crewman
misses the boat . . .

      Tangier Sound, off Deal Island

skipjacks
parading along the
starting line,
waiting for the gun
and a chance to run

      Tangier Sound, off Deal Island

rounding the first mark,
dueling with
the *City of Crisfield*,
she makes the mark but
we pursue and overtake

      Tangier Sound, off Deal Island

Slow Motion

chasing the second mark,
a minefield of crab pots;
the *City of Crisfield*
runs far out, giving ground
to gain the best point of sail

        Tangier Sound, off Deal Island

at the second mark,
the *City of Crisfield* flying in
on a broad reach,
we cross her bow and
try to steal her wind

        Tangier Sound, off Deal Island

skipjacks
swerving around the mark
at full speed,
white knights
with lances set

        Tangier Sound, off Deal Island

The Log of a Chesapeake Bay Skipjack

we can't catch her . . .
the *City of Crisfield,*
rounds the last mark

    Tangier Sound, off Deal Island

wind nearly dead—
the taunt of the
City of Crisfield
running wing and wing
just ahead of us

    Tangier Sound, off Deal Island

not waiting for
the Awards Banquet,
our second place boat
heads north to the place
where she is always first

    Tangier Sound

Slow Motion

our wake—
rolling into
nothingness

Hooper Strait

small freight—
black-winged gulls
in the shipping channel

Hooper Strait

white dog-tooth violet—
a ketch on the horizon

Hooper Strait

The Log of a Chesapeake Bay Skipjack

Wingate, Maryland—
the harbor
crossed by the
bridge of
the Milky Way

Wingate

starbow—
the Milky Way
horizon to horizon

Wingate

an old skipjack
comes home to the place
of her birth,
and all the old people
come out to meet her

Wingate

Slow Motion

Honga River
boathook dredgers . . .
another tradition
passed from an old captain
to a younger captain

Wingate

a screen porch—
genuine hospitality
this mosquito night
I settle to sleep
on the veranda

Captain Ozylee's Porch, Wingate

cautious about strangers,
the cat inspects us
before granting permission
to sleep on his floor

Captain Ozylee's Porch, Wingate

The Log of a Chesapeake Bay Skipjack

Honga River Boathook Dredgers

The Skipjack Martha Lewis *was born in Wingate, Maryland. Skipjacks are people, so they don't get 'built'—they are born. They spend their lives working, and then they die. No matter where a skipjack works or how long she is gone, her hometown is still her hometown.*

Captain Ozylee Lewis (retired) and his wife Naomi were sitting up waiting to meet us. They had already heard the outcome of the races—the grapevine is in full service on the Eastern Shore—so congratulated us and invited us in. We sat for hours with both of them while they showed us pictures and told us stories. Captain Ozylee is the son of Captain Jim Lewis, Martha's first captain. Hearing that we were going to sleep on deck, they invited us to sleep in the screened porch of their small house. The house isn't air-conditioned so the porch was the coolest room. Having screens would save us from the Honga River mosquitos, so we were glad to accept.

Next morning when we were trying to depart, we had a horde of visitors. Or what passes for a 'horde' in a town composed of two churches and seventeen crab boats. They had to come see **Martha***. Another skipjack had also spent the night in the harbor, but was not a Wingate boat, so received only cursory attention. Dan Lewis, Ozylee's grandson, was part of our crew, and we discovered we couldn't send him on errands because he got stopped every thirty feet by somebody who wanted to talk to him.*

Slow Motion

<u>September 4, Tuesday</u>

two skipjacks
in the harbor,
an old woman tells us
about the one who
didn't come home

Wingate

they go into
the marshes to die
these old boats,
their wooden hearts
rotten with neglect

Wingate, talking about Deal Island

leaving the harbor
not a single cloud—
just a ring of
yellow haze
around the boat

Honga River

The Log of a Chesapeake Bay Skipjack

why isn't
Sharp Island Light
as famous as
the Leaning Tower of Pisa?
and for the same reason?

    Sharp Island Shoals

rush hour—
three powerboats
in the Severn River—
a weary skipjack
turns her head to harbor

    Severn River

hungry, hot, and tired
nearly broke
yearning for
cheap food
and a shower

    Annapolis

Slow Motion

four days underway—
yearning for a
Blondie sandwich
at the Ritz
of Havre de Grace

Annapolis

beyond the
night heron's silhouette,
a cruise ship

'Ego Alley' Spa Creek, Annapolis

a night heron
and an old workboat
settle down
at their weathered pilings
away from the yachts

Annapolis

The Log of a Chesapeake Bay Skipjack

Annapolis

Another close encounter with people trying to help. A skipjack isn't a yacht and can't be treated like one. Two fellows associated with a rather fine vessel kindly took our lines and tied them off, thereby complicating our docking procedures. All the same, we managed in spite of their help. This time we got our shower tokens before the Harbormaster closed: one each. We then walked a mile or so to an Irish cop café, had dinner, and walked back. Captain Greg bought an expensive cigar, and we got ice for our coolers.

The party atmosphere and traffic of Labor Day weekend had subsided. We were getting tired. Sleeping on board a skipjack is like camping, but with fewer amenities. This time we tied down the squeaking bumper board on the piling and slept the better for it. Next morning we were all up at dawn's first gleam. Working briskly because we were weary and wanted to go home, we departed without fanfare or regrets.

Slow Motion

September 5, Wednesday

dawn—
stars bright in a navy blue sky
over Annapolis

Annapolis

Naval Academy
falling astern,
the old skipjack
steams north
to winter

Severn River, off Annapolis

astern,
the dome of
the Statehouse
shrinking
this amber morning

Severn River, off Annapolis

The Log of a Chesapeake Bay Skipjack

Thomas Point Light—
an old friend on
the Chesapeake Bay

    Severn River

Poole Island . . .
the white cylinder of
the lighthouse
as small and distant
as my thoughts of home

    approaching Poole Island from the south

another lighthouse
by Donahoo; I recognize
the white cylinder,
the black cap,
the vigil of centuries

    approaching Poole Island from the south

Slow Motion

who was he,
builder of
lighthouses,
this man who
lit the centuries?

off Poole Island

I call it 'Avalon'
even though I know
it's littered with
unspent ordinance
and boyhood dreams

off Poole Island

a dark shadow
on the waters,
Poole Island,
land of mysteries
I will never know

off Poole Island

The Log of a Chesapeake Bay Skipjack

the debate:
fuel enough, or not?
I stick a stick
in the gas tank
to measure

> *middle of the Chesapeake Bay*

off Turkey Point,
wearing my hat
on my knee
to save it from
further sunburn

> *off Turkey Point*

almost home . . .
Turkey Point Lighthouse
a sliver of white
against the forest

> *off Turkey Point*

Slow Motion

cormorants
black arrows diving
into the other world

        off Fishing Battery Island

adrift in a sea of clouds
their white perfection
all around our hull

        off Fishing Battery Island

coming home
lowering the mains'l,
downhaul in my left hand,
halyard in my right,
not enough hands!

        off Havre de Grace

The Log of a Chesapeake Bay Skipjack

wrapping my legs
around the bowsprit
while I tie the jib,
the blueness of the sky
reflected below me

Havre de Grace

shirtless
in the autumn dusk,
my skin drinking up
the last heat
of summer

Havre de Grace

no horizon
but the sea,
no dream
but tomorrow

Perryville

Slow Motion

day after,
mal de disembarkation
   my bed slowly swaying

           Perryville

I'm not
at the end of
my rope,
but I can see it
from here

           Perryville

Interlude : the Lantern Queen

Whenever the opportunity presents itself, I avail myself of the opportunity to board other historic vessels, as a crew member if I can finagle it, as a curious guest when I can get away with it, or as a tourist, if there is no other way. Accordingly, when the crew of the Martha Lewis *was invited for a cruise aboard the* Lantern Queen*, the dinner cruise paddlewheeler that had been out of commission to undergo restoration for many months, I went. Being the nosy sort of guest that I am, I poked my head in the pilot house and asked permission to visit, which was granted. Professional courtesy: historic vessels all share the same mission, and so there is a fellowship among them.*

The Lantern Queen *is a steel hulled reproduction of a small paddlewheeler, the likes of which used to haul passengers and freight up and down the Chesapeake Bay during the age of steam. Once upon a time steamboats even tied up at the Bow (now Bow Street) in downtown Elkton, but the Elk River has silted to the point you can wade across it. The same fate has overtaken many small towns on the Chesapeake and the vessels that used to serve them.*

Slow Motion

<u>October 13, Saturday</u>

working all day
then changing clothes
so fast I forget my belt—
my son and I
run for the gangplank

Havre de Grace

"closed for restoration
~~open September~~
open October"
on the window of
the paddlewheel boat

Havre de Grace

the dead rise
and so do old boats—
the *Lantern Queen*
back at
her usual dock

Havre de Grace

The Log of a Chesapeake Bay Skipjack

white walls
red paddlewheels
black capped smokestacks . . .
a bright oasis
in the river of night

        Havre de Grace

standing clear,
watching the deckhands
raise the gangplank—
for once I am
a passenger

        aboard the Lantern Queen, Havre de Grace

officers
white shirts and epaulettes
me in cargo pants
and sweater—
a moment of envy

        aboard the Lantern Queen, Havre de Grace

Slow Motion

hanging over
the *Lantern Queen's* taffrail,
I get a face
full of spray
from her paddlewheels

        aboard the Lantern Queen, Havre de Grace

watching one
paddlewheel churn forward
and the other backward . . .
how hard we must work
just to hold our place in the world

        aboard the Lantern Queen, Havre de Grace

uncharted territory—
the little sternwheeler
slips under
the bridge where
our mast cannot fit

        aboard the Lantern Queen, Susquehanna River

The Log of a Chesapeake Bay Skipjack

a river of stars . . .
a single red one
on the bow of the barge

> *aboard the Lantern Queen, Susquehanna River*

Certificate of Inspection—
I am the only diner
that pauses to read
the particulars of
the host vessel

> *aboard the Lantern Queen*

the oysterboat crew
dining amid lace curtains
in the saloon
of the sternwheeler,
the *Lantern Queen*

> *aboard the Lantern Queen*

Slow Motion

not like
dinner ashore:
life jackets
in the false ceiling

        aboard the Lantern Queen

Louie Armstrong
serenades the diners—
the darkness
of the river outside

        aboard the Lantern Queen

the sudden clatter
of a buoy against the
steel hull—
grinning because
it's not my problem

        aboard the Lantern Queen, Susquehanna River

The Log of a Chesapeake Bay Skipjack

all through dinner
the clatter of the engine
I miss our sails

      aboard the Lantern Queen, Susquehanna River

on the upper deck
of the paddlewheeler,
I point out the Big Dipper
and teach my son
how to find the North Star

      aboard the Lantern Queen, Susquehanna River

the rattle of gunfire
in the dark hills . . .
this riverboat night

      aboard the Lantern Queen, Susquehanna River

Slow Motion

the lights of the quarry
even at this hour of the night

> *aboard the Lantern Queen, Susquehanna River*

Even Further South

In October, I crewed aboard the Martha Lewis *for her trip the Watermen's Festival in Crisfield. That was even further south than Deal Island and took a pair of ten hour days to get there. We stopped at Tilghman's Island overnight. The days were pleasantly mild and the nights weren't as cold as the trip to Deal. However, it was foggy, damp, and rainy for part of the trip. As usual, we met watermen wherever we went who had worked on* Martha.

A striking detail of the conversations was how watermen referenced time: they spoke about working on Martha *"back when winters were actually cold." Indeed, as late as the 1950s, ice was a menace to skipjacks whose wooden hulls could be crushed by the huge floes on the Bay. When I tell young people that the Upper Bay used to freeze over and that ice cut from the Bay was Maryland's second largest export, they look at me in disbelief, but their grandparents nod and talk about how they used to walk across the ice from one side of the Bay to the other. Global warming is manifesting in the Chesapeake Bay about twice as fast as the rest of the world. Inland folks might be able to argue about it, but not watermen.*

Slow Motion

October 17, Wednesday

last night
the cries of wild geese,
this morning,
I follow them south

    off Havre de Grace

glassy water
and a pink blush
in the eastern sky,
a brand new barge
pushing up the channel

    off Havre de Grace

half a red disk
rising
from the fog bank . . .
we pass
Fishing Battery Light

    off Fishing Battery Light

The Log of a Chesapeake Bay Skipjack

pant legs
damp with dew
autumn morning

    off Fishing Battery Light

the first deadrise
checking her lines,
crab pots empty

    off North East River

the salt line
as far north as
Spesutia Island . . .
watermen desperate
for crabs

    off North East River

Slow Motion

for a moment
I gaze over
the starboard rail . . .
when I return,
my seat covered with dew

        off North East River

passing Spesutia Island,
the thump of ordinance
and the red insignia of
military patrol boats
in the early morning

        off Aberdeen Proving Ground

a blue sky
above the grey fog waters
a white skipjack
steaming south
at seven knots

        off Aberdeen Proving Ground

The Log of a Chesapeake Bay Skipjack

things invisible to see—
Poole Island
lost in the mist

        off Sassafras River

the mouth of
Still Pond Creek
breathing
fog onto the
reaches of the Bay

        off Still Pond Creek

working the Bay:
a tugboat pushes two barges
up the channel

        off Worton Creek

Slow Motion

a matched set:
red and green buoys
and black-winged gulls

       off Worton Creek

seaweed
wrapped around
a crab float . . .
how we cling to
little things

       off Worton Creek

the waterman's map
he raises his arm and points:
    Havre de Grace is the fingertip
    Annapolis is the elbow
    and Crisfield is the armpit

       off Worton Creek

The Log of a Chesapeake Bay Skipjack

autumn
on the Chesapeake:
an encyclopedia of grey

    off Poole Island

the fog
slowly burning off,
the dim reds
of autumn
on Poole Island

    off Poole Island

first nap
of the Indian summer day
smokestacks
of Sparrows Point
in the distance

    south of Poole Island

Slow Motion

cutting through
crab pots,
some of them
turn into gulls
and fly away

        off Tolchester Beach

every day
on the water
is the first day—
never will the wind
blow over the same shore

        off Tolchester Beach

no sailboats—
to see the world
from the deck
of a working boat
in autumn

        off Tolchester Beach

The Log of a Chesapeake Bay Skipjack

rocking horse swells—
the pony boat
bobs her head
as she canters
over the water

       off Tolchester Beach

the blue bowl
of the sky full
of silver light
Indian summer
on the Chesapeake Bay

       off Tolchester Beach

white workboats
the only color
on this heron-blue sea
wider than the dreams
of either shore

       off Tolchester Beach

Slow Motion

a black youth
in oversize overalls
tossing crab pots
from the roof of
his father's deadrise

      off Tolchester Beach

my turn at the helm
just the bay,
the boat, and
a yellow butterfly
this autumn day

      approaching the Bay Bridge

the stocky bulk of
Magothy Light—
dwarfed by freighters
heading for
the Bay Bridge

      approaching the Bay Bridge

The Log of a Chesapeake Bay Skipjack

all courses converge
on the center span
of the Bay Bridge—
tugs, freighters, schooners,
skipjacks, powerboats

      approaching the Bay Bridge

in the middle of the Bay,
using the captain's cell phone
to look up the words to
"Seven Old Ladies
Got Stuck in the Lavatory"

      off Severn River

seagulls
whitewashing
Bloody Point Light

      Bloody Point Light

Slow Motion

pound net
in the mouth of
Poplar Harbor
a cormorant
on every piling

approaching Poplar Island Narrows

Green Marsh Point—
a mansion so huge
it's marked on
charts as
an aid to navigation

Poplar Island Narrows

three markers
lead into
Knapp Narrows,
each with
its osprey nest

approaching Knapp Narrows

The Log of a Chesapeake Bay Skipjack

a perfect maneuver:
I throw the bowline and
the boat pivots on it,
coming to rest pointing
back the way she came

        Knapp Narrows, Tilghman Island

Tilghman Island,
the Bridge Restaurant's sign:
    Dockage
    Diners Free
    Visitors $10 per foot

        Knapp Narrows, Tilghman Island

sunset
spiders rappelling
out of the rigging

        Knapp Narrows, Tilghman Island

The Log of a Chesapeake Bay Skipjack

Monsters in the Mist

    My second trip down the Bay was longer, cooler, and damper than the first. It was a lot more like work the second time around. Our crew was in good spirits, cracking jokes, listening to the radio, and even singing bawdy songs. We had a great deal of fog and mist, which puts the Bay in a whole other perspective. Freighters and frigates loom out of the fog like mythical creatures being born in the dawn of time. The wreck of the North Carolina, *so prominent in clear weather, was hardly identifiable as more than a vague, ship-like shape. Yet as picturesque as the view was, it posed a danger as well: A small wooden sailboat is nearly invisible to the radar that the large ships use. At such times it's a comfort to be aboard a skipjack, knowing that her shallow hull permits her to sail shoal waters where monsters dare not tread.*

Slow Motion

October 18, Thursday

predawn
the morning star
the only star
left in the
rosy east

Knapp Narrows, Tilghman Island

5 am rush hour:
deadrise after deadrise
diesels roaring
the clatter of
drawbridge alarms

Knapp Narrows, Tilghman Island

an Eastern Shore
watermen's town:
rising before
Orion and his hounds
have gone to bed

Knapp Narrows, Tilghman Island

The Log of a Chesapeake Bay Skipjack

not yet dawn
on Tilghman's Island—
a waterman returns
with bushel baskets
full of crabs

leaving Knapp Narrows, Tilghman Island

pound nets—
too early in the dawn
even for cormorants

leaving Knapp Narrows, Tilghman Island

expensive houses—
they want to
get away from it all,
but they
bring it all with them

Tilghman Island

Slow Motion

warm in town—
once we come out
of the Narrows,
I dig in my kit
for a sweater

      off Tilghman Island

clouds streaked with glory
an autumn dawn
on the Chesapeake Bay

      off Tilghman Island

the sun
finally appears
above Tilghman Island,
shorebirds gather
at the pound nets

      off Tilghman Island

The Log of a Chesapeake Bay Skipjack

rolling swells
spray breaking every
tenth wave
the cries of seagulls
scatter around us

      off Tilghman Island

the leaning tower
of the Chesapeake—
Sharp Island Light
dead ahead
on the horizon

      off Sharp Island Light

Sharp's Island—
nothing left
but stories

      off Sharp Island Light

Slow Motion

8 am
hot chocolate
the captain
compliments us
on our departure

        off Sharp Island Light

eating breakfast
in shifts—
the Calvert Cliffs
come into view
over the starboard rail

        off Sharp Island Light

a sweater,
hot chocolate, and sun—
I'm now sufficiently warm
on the deck of
an autumn skipjack

        off Sharp Island Light

The Log of a Chesapeake Bay Skipjack

workboat etiquette:
wiping my mouth
on my sweater sleeve

        south of Sharp Island Light

toilet paper
in short supply
I hold it
a little longer

        south of Sharp Island Light

running down
the 'false channel'
toward the James Islands . . .
it's good to be
a skipjack

        False Channel, approaching James Islands

Slow Motion

just after breakfast,
a container ship and
crab boat
the only company
in the sweep of dawn

        off James Islands

James Islands
dim in the eastern mist
this gaunt silence

        off James Islands

shearwaters
soaring through the haze
of an October morning

        off James Islands

The Log of a Chesapeake Bay Skipjack

big water—
no north
no south
Calvert Cliffs
faint in the distance

        off James Islands

grey water
grey shore
grey clouds
white workboats
the only color

        off Taylor Island

humidity
the ginger 'snaps'
are now ginger 'bends'

        off Taylor Island

Slow Motion

the captain,
the helm, and the navigator,
intent on discussing
DaVinci's inventions,
nearly snag a crab pot

    off Taylor Island

the deadrise
Endless Summer
comes along side
and delivers a message
to our captain

    off Barren Island

wearing *Lady Katie's*
mast hoops, of course
we agree to help
install a new bowsprit
on the *Katie*

    off Barren Island

The Log of a Chesapeake Bay Skipjack

still passing
Calvert Cliffs
thirty miles of
red stone bones
capped with green

       off Barren Island

frigates steaming north
their mist-grey hulls
faint in the autumn haze

       off Barren Island

the wideness
of the Chesapeake . . .
only a few islands
visible at
Holland Island Bar Light

       off Holland Island Bar Light

Slow Motion

the western shore
has vanished,
and with it,
life as
most people know it

        off Holland Island Bar Light

clouds
ladders of light
descending from
the heavens
to the sea

        off Holland Island Bar Light

the black
and white diamonds
of Holland Island Bar Light—
this too
belongs to cormorants

        off Holland Island Bar Light

The Log of a Chesapeake Bay Skipjack

the jib swaying
and the shrouds talking
as the skipjack rolls
in a beam sea
in Kedges Strait

      Kedges Strait

the great expanse
of the Chesapeake Bay
absolutely empty
but for one skipjack
wet with spray

      Kedges Strait

the white tower
of Solomons Lump Light,
tiny between
the grey
sky and water

      Kedges Strait

Slow Motion

Solomons Lump Light
off-center
on its caisson,
the square tower
poised as if to dive

> *Kedges Strait*

a caisson lighthouse
once occupied,
but not even a
piece of riprap
to stand on

> *Kedges Strait*

green slate—
the waters of
Tangier Sound

> *Tangier Sound*

The Log of a Chesapeake Bay Skipjack

Tangier Sound
scraps of islands
the only land

Tangier Sound

islands
in the Chesapeake—
a hundred years of
global warming
and they will vanish

Tangier Sound

six sailors
in a vast and
empty sea—
the joy of
being alone

Tangier Sound

Slow Motion

broad enough
to see the curve
of the earth,
the waters of
Tangier Sound

       Tangier Sound

humans can never be
anything but visitors
in the great green sea

       Tangier Sound

an empty fuel tank . . .
we drift a little
in Tangier Sound

       Tangier Sound

Red Cap Creek

The crew of the Martha Lewis *was invited to a dinner hosted by Randy and Smarro George then given overnight hospitality at their home, a 1720s plantation house,* Williams Conquest, *which they have beautifully restored, placing it and its 450 acres into a historic preservation trust. The plantation is situated on Galen's Greek, named after the area's only Civil War general, who lived along its banks, but it was formerly known as Red Cap Creek and still is to oldtimers.*

On Friday morning before we piled into Randy's pickup truck for the ride back to the marina, he invited us out on his three log sailing canoe, the Ruby. Built in 1895, she is a workboat used for hand tonging oysters and other chores. The log sailing canoe is a craft peculiar to the Chesapeake Bay, having been evolved by the early colonists from the Native dugout. The Ruby is a three log canoe, meaning three logs were laid side by side and hollowed out and joined. She has a single raked mast and sports a skipjack rig. In 1912 she was 'modernized' with the addition of a small engine, started by giving the flywheel a good spin.

Slow Motion

October 19 Friday

southern breakfast
asparagus fresh from the garden,
eggs and bacon
served on broad china plates
in an old plantation house

      Williams Conquest, Red Cap Creek

as night
surrenders to dawn,
a slim mast
emerges from the mist
of Red Cap Creek

      Williams Conquest, Red Cap Creek

the marshes
turning brown
as the *Ruby*
motors out of
Red Cap Creek

      Red Cap Creek

The Log of a Chesapeake Bay Skipjack

could a man
ever be happier than
when he sees
houses sinking into the mist
as he sails away?

       Red Cap Creek

at the tiller of the *Ruby*
a sailing canoe
of three logs,
feeling the age
of the Chesapeake Bay

       Big Annemessex River

a new appreciation
for 'low,'
the *Ruby's* gunwale
inches above
the creek

       Big Annemessex River

Slow Motion

an open boat
beneath an open sky,
the sailing canoe
slips through the marshes
of the Big Annemessex River

Big Annemessex River

a little white boat
always busy
never doing anything
always going somewhere
happy never to arrive

Big Annemessex River

a waking dream:
marshes wending their curves
just for me
and one little sailboat
on an autumn day

Big Annemessex River

The Log of a Chesapeake Bay Skipjack

pointing high
into the wind—
the rush of water
and a fine thin
wake left behind

      Big Annemessex River

the railroad barge
rusted and decrepit
nothing now
but a landmark
for a single white sailboat

      Red Cap Creek

as Mole when he first
beheld the Water Rat's boat,
so was I entranced
by that slim white hull
and her raked mast

      Red Cap Creek

Slow Motion

down in Mary's Land
the seas are broad and sweet,
all the sailboats free,
and Indian summer lasts forever
on Red Cap Creek

Red Cap Creek

Crisfield Watermen's Festival

The Crisfield Waterman's Festival is only two years old and is an example of a small town trying to create tourism out of heritage. The festival featured all-you-can-eat crabs and other foods, plus oystershucking and crabpicking contests. Native Americans gave an exhibition of traditional dances and reminded the audience that the Natives are the original watermen. Indeed, Europeans in America were at first loathe to eat crabs, regarding them as being some sort of giant insect. Now the blue crab is the Maryland State Crustacean and a staple of the diet.

The Skipjack Martha Lewis docked at A Pier on the opposite side of Somers Cove from the festivities, with a fence and screening in between, making her hard to see and a long walk to reach. Of the hundreds who attended the festival, only a few hardy souls made the trek around to our side of the cove. They included several watermen who graced us with their personal stories and jokes.

In her fifty-plus years of working life, she has carried many crewmen and is slowly outliving them. Martha is a museum on the water, but more than that, she is a time capsule of a way of life that is fast vanishing between the twin pressures of ecological change and the urbanization/suburbanization of Maryland's shore.

Slow Motion

<u>October 19 Friday</u>

watermen's humor:
sending
the new hand
to fill up
the centerboard well

   Crisfield, Maryland

watermen's humor:
sending
the new guy
to fetch thirty feet
of shore line

   Crisfield, Maryland

watermen's humor:
sending
the new guy
to bring
a crab stretcher

   Crisfield, Maryland

The Log of a Chesapeake Bay Skipjack

watermen's lingo:
dish ca'm—
so calm it wouldn't
ruffle piss
in a dish pan

        Crisfield, Maryland

not quite understanding,
a tourist asks if
"Martha Lewis"
and "Harvey DeGrace"
own the skipjack

        Crisfield, Maryland

I'm not saying
they had money,
but there was
a crystal chandelier
in the bathroom

        Crisfield, Maryland

Slow Motion

a black man
tells me about
his ancestors,
cooks aboard
skipjacks of yore

        Somers Cove, Crisfield, Maryland

black watermen—
sometimes
it feels like
we are living
in parallel universes

        Somers Cove, Crisfield, Maryland

wherever we go,
an ex-waterman
comes to tell us
"She looks good" and
about his days on board

        Somers Cove, Crisfield, Maryland

The Log of a Chesapeake Bay Skipjack

a small skill—
taking pride
in throwing the bowline
and usually
catching my piling

        Somers Cove, Crisfield, Maryland

a cowboy flip
and the bowline
comes free—
the fuel dock
slipping away

        Somers Cove, Crisfield, Maryland

after dark
Friday night
out of season
the cruise ship
departs empty

        Somers Cove, Crisfield, Maryland

Slow Motion

dance band
on the *Martha Lewis*,
guitars on the foredeck
Friday night
in Somers Cove

        Somers Cove, Crisfield, Maryland

in a state
of inebriation
I contemplate the chasm
between ship and shore
and make the leap

        Somers Cove, Crisfield, Maryland

a few vague stars—
although drunk,
the sailors
gaze up
in reverence

        Somers Cove, Crisfield, Maryland

The Log of a Chesapeake Bay Skipjack

intoxicated—
stealing toilet paper
for the boat

> *Somers Cove, Crisfield, Maryland*

the rum's all gone
the boat sleeping
the moon, too,
sunk in the obscurity
of night

> *Somers Cove, Crisfield, Maryland*

sobering up
before I sleep—
a little regret
in the middle
of many more

> *Somers Cove, Crisfield, Maryland*

Slow Motion

midnight on the water,
the world the size
of a wooden deck

      Somers Cove, Crisfield, Maryland

mild weather—
yet the dark warning
of clouds
piling up
beyond the mast

      Somers Cove, Crisfield, Maryland

it sounds
like popcorn popping
all night long . . .
the snap of the flags
in the freshening breeze

      Somers Cove, Crisfield, Maryland

The Log of a Chesapeake Bay Skipjack

water slaps
under the docks,
never once
does the wind
leave our rigging alone

       Somers Cove, Crisfield, Maryland

clouds
devour the moon—
the dock lights
no protection against
the threat of storm

       Somers Cove, Crisfield, Maryland

I ought to sleep
while I can—
a forecast of storms
in the blue night

       Somers Cove, Crisfield, Maryland

Slow Motion

threat of storms—
then the western moon
breaking through
the clouds
over Somers Cove

Somers Cove, Crisfield, Maryland

journal open
beneath the harbor cover
tonight
I am Crisfield's watchman

Somers Cove, Crisfield, Maryland

a folded
Indian blanket
for a pillow,
sleeping on deck
October night

Somers Cove, Crisfield, Maryland

Chesapeake Dawn

After our interlude in Crisfield, it was time to make the long trek back home. The storms never materialized and we didn't even get rained on that night. Up before Orion and his hounds went to bed, we followed them out the channel to the west. When they bedded down for the day, we watched a glorious dawn circling all around us: east, south, west, and north. When there are no trees and houses in the way, a golden pink glow forms a complete circle on the horizon of the sea. Whether this is a characteristic of the oceans or just the Chesapeake Bay I do not know, but it is one of God's gifts granted to those who work the water.

Slow Motion

October 20, Saturday

Venus
bright in a halo
of haze,
dawn in
Crisfield's harbor

Somers Cove, Crisfield, Maryland

a sad sight
dawn and
deadrises
sitting empty
in the harbor

Somers Cove, Crisfield, Maryland

headboat fishing
another crabber
changes careers

Somers Cove, Crisfield, Maryland

The Log of a Chesapeake Bay Skipjack

predawn
throwing the bowline
barefoot

        Somers Cove, Crisfield, Maryland

flat calm
Orion and his hounds
leading the way
to the western sea
this morning

        Somers Cove, Crisfield, Maryland

Old Island
once a menhaden
factory—
now just a chimney
amid the waste

        leaving Crisfield, Maryland

Slow Motion

a pencil line
of land
drawn between
the sea and the sky
seagulls adrift

       leaving Crisfield, Maryland

bird condo
fifty cormorants
perched on
the warning marker
in Crisfield channel

       leaving Crisfield, Maryland

Janes Island Light—
an old black caisson
supports
a new black and white
set of diamonds

       off Janes Island Light

The Log of a Chesapeake Bay Skipjack

dawn—
pink clouds on
every horizon

Tangier Sound

cold wet feet—
I surrender to autumn
and put on my shoes

Tangier Sound

fair morning
an aqua slate sea
a band of mackerel clouds
broad across
the middle of the bay

Tangier Sound

Slow Motion

sunrays
fanning down
between the clouds,
a yellow shimmer
on the water

        Tangier Sound

last seen
least regretted
the Crisfield condos

        Tangier Sound

if you build it,
they won't come . . .
Crisfield condos

        Tangier Sound

The Log of a Chesapeake Bay Skipjack

the skipjack
with her sails raised:
taller
and whiter than
Solomons Lump Light

off Solomons Lump Light, Tangier Sound

the sun
briefly breaks free
of the eastern clouds—
for a moment
the warmth of Indian summer

off Solomons Lump Light, Tangier Sound

the square tower
of Solomons Lump Light
off center
on its rusty red
caisson

off Solomons Lump Light, Tangier Sound

Slow Motion

daylight
and fair weather
an old wreck
visible
off the port bow

> *Kedges Strait*

Janes Island
pelicans dark
as winter
hunting under
our bow

> *Kedges Strait*

Saturday morning—
the slim white triangles
of pleasure boats
counting down the days
of Indian summer

> *coming out of Kedges Strait*

The Log of a Chesapeake Bay Skipjack

Saturday in
Indian summer—
sailboat
after sailboat
winging down the Bay

    coming out of Kedges Strait

throwing spray
as we bounce
over the waves—
Calvert Cliffs
ten thousand years old

    off Calvert Cliffs

a wall of spray
sweeps across
the mid-deck—
we alter course to take
the waves head on

    off Calvert Cliffs

Slow Motion

raising the hatch
just in time
to catch a faceful of spray
and an earful of
Frank Sinatra

> *off Calvert Cliffs*

rocking horse waves—
safe from the spray
in the lee of
the winder box,
I take a nap

> *off Calvert Cliffs*

the only dry
nap spot,
another crewman
claims it
when I wake

> *approaching Sharp's Island Light*

The Log of a Chesapeake Bay Skipjack

fine on
the starboard bow,
the leaning tower
of Sharp's Island Light
and a tall sailboat

    approaching Sharp's Island Light

two sailboats
set in the silver sea,
a white sun overhead

    off Sharp's Island Light

red autumn
or green spring,
it doesn't matter—
a boat's the only
place to be

    off Sharp's Island Light

Slow Motion

riding
the pitching foredeck
watching for crab pots
salt spray clinging
to a week-old beard

approaching Knapp Narrows

a fancy maneuver
to dock the skipjack—
the line fouls
and I miss the throw . . .
we brush the bulwark

Knapp Narrows, Tilghman Island

rich people get
nervous as the skipjack
swings out of control
and her bowsprit
threatens the yachts

Knapp Narrows, Tilghman Island

The Log of a Chesapeake Bay Skipjack

second try—
the wet rope slides
through my gloves
when I try to pin it
to the samson post

Knapp Narrows, Tilghman Island

thirty tons
of boat swinging wide—
my glove
trapped against
the samson post

Knapp Narrows, Tilghman Island

desperate,
yanking my hand
as hard as I can
to free it from
the samson post

Knapp Narrows, Tilghman Island

Slow Motion

finally
the bowline tight
around the samson post,
cinching her
back to the dock

Knapp Narrows, Tilghman Island

the ache of my arm
from fingertips
to shoulderblade
     the only damage
     our eagle's broken nose

Knapp Narrows, Tilghman Island

our eagle—
not the first
waterman to have
his nose broken
in a tussle

Knapp Narrows, Tilghman Island

The Log of a Chesapeake Bay Skipjack

Breakfast at the Bridge

Once again we were granted permission to tie up at the Bridge Restaurant's dock in Knapp Narrows in exchange for having dinner there. We had a special request of the cook that night: we had forgotten a spatula and planned to make pancakes for breakfast. Since the restaurant would not open until hours after we had left, our request to borrow a spatula required negotiation. The resulting agreement was that we would leave a sample of whatever was being cooked with the spatula along with the spatula on the restaurant's doorstep for the cook to find in the morning. Presumably he did, although there was a large polydactyl cat who came to beg his breakfast of us that morning, so I cannot rule out the possibility of feline piracy. Next year when we return we will have to ask.

Slow Motion

<u>October 21, Sunday</u>

a polydactyl cat
walks the bulwark—
he, too,
is the offspring
of sailors

Knapp Narrows, Tilghman Island

at the dock
an orange cat
with a white bib
inquires of us
for his breakfast

Knapp Narrows, Tilghman Island

making breakfast
with a spatula borrowed
from the restaurant,
leaving it where
the cook will find it

Knapp Narrows, Tilghman Island

The Log of a Chesapeake Bay Skipjack

cold on the water,
the autumn sun
no more than
a yellow premonition
on the horizon

Knapp Narrows, Tilghman Island

Poplar Island
low flat and weedy
in the west—
obviously not named
for its trees

Poplar Harbor

crab pot hell . . .
red pots, blue pots, black pots,
invisible pots
we cut the engine
to save the propellor

Poplar Harbor

Slow Motion

dawn,
finally warm enough
to eat—
I go below
and grab my cereal

       off Bloody Point Light

in the mouth of
the Severn River
a pair of warships
grey mountains
anchored in the sea

       south of the Bay Bridge

the metal struts
of the Bay Bridge
singing in the sun

       under the Bay Bridge

The Log of a Chesapeake Bay Skipjack

coming through
the Bay Bridge,
the wake of
a container ship
rocks a wooden sailboat

under the Bay Bridge

lunch at the wheel,
taking bites between
crab pots,
steering with a hand
and two feet

off Kent Island, north of the Bay Bridge

after lunch,
Billie Holiday
singing in my ear
a nap on top
of the lifejackets

off Kent Island, north of the Bay Bridge

Slow Motion

smogbank
on the western shore—
Baltimore's pollution
blown all the way
to the Eastern Shore

      off Kent Island, north of the Bay Bridge

smogbank off Baltimore—
even the water turns brown

      off Baltimore

Baltimore's smog
can't dim the beauty
of a white-sailed ketch
coasting along
Tolchester Beach

      off Tolchester Beach

The Log of a Chesapeake Bay Skipjack

quiet time
mending the boom lift—
weaving an eye splice
without the benefit
of a marlinspike

       off Tolchester Beach

passing Poole Island
the first range light appears:
the home stretch at last
thirty miles, five hours,
then a shower

       off Poole Island

the white sail
of a pleasure boat
coasting along
the bluffs of
Worton Creek

       off Worton Creek

Slow Motion

red, white, and yellow
powerboats
roaring past
the skipjack
with her sails set

    off Aberdeen Proving Ground

smoke billowing up
from the woods
of Aberdeen—
ordinance testing
at the proving ground

    off Aberdeen Proving Ground

Turkey Point
in the distance—
the heart quickens
in home waters

    off Turkey Point

The Log of a Chesapeake Bay Skipjack

Turkey Point Light:
that white tower
means 'home' to me,
even if port is
hours away

    off Turkey Point

late afternoon
a line of pleasure boats
heading home

    off Fishing Battery Light

passing Sand Island,
the Redneck Yacht Club
in full session

    off Fishing Battery Light

Slow Motion

this point,
that lighthouse,
another island . . .
all of them
leading home

   off Fishing Battery Light

the pale blue arch
of the Hatem Bridge
never looked so beautiful—
we come up the bay
after five days of autumn

   Havre de Grace Channel

journey's end . . .
a narrow channel
leads to the marina
from whence
we ventured long ago

   Marina Channel

The Log of a Chesapeake Bay Skipjack

wives and husbands
on the sunny dock,
waving at the skipjack,
each eye searching for
the figure they love best

City Marina, Havre de Grace

make fast the lines
on their own pilings,
flake down the jib,
heave out the luggage,
shake hands goodbye

. . . for now

City Marina, Havre de Grace

reluctantly
returning to shore—
too tired to even dream
about a shallow creek
and a log canoe

Perryville, Maryland

Slow Motion

this plain door
holds the emptiness
of a place left behind;
I feel no welcome
as I cross its threshold

Perryville, Maryland

two days home—
landsick already

Perryville, Maryland

Shore Leave: Making a Living on the Land

Alas for me, nobody makes a living 'drudging arsters,' as they say in the Eastern Shore. I'd rather rather be cold and work hard, get up early, and leave the shore behind than to trudge off to my marginally paying job at the Wal-Mart. All my time aboard the Skipjack Martha Lewis *is volunteered, squeezed in once a week during the warm weather and whenever I can during cold.*

Crewing on board, reefing out seams, crawling through a cold bilge painting on preservative, going up the mast in a bosun's chair—I've done it all, and expect to keep doing it as long as my body allows it.

Slow Motion

<u>November 2-8</u>

"fall back"
the working man's
extra hour of sleep

           Perryville, Maryland

another thing
to bear—Christmas
in a discount store
a job
is a job

           Elkton, Maryland

bomb threat
at the Wal-mart—
I resign myself
to the working conditions
of the working man

           Elkton, Maryland

The Log of a Chesapeake Bay Skipjack

working at Wal-mart,
I miss the sky
the most—
looking up, nothing but
girders and ceiling tiles

Elkton, Maryland

"skylights"
they call them,
but no sign
of sky beyond
the frosted plastic

Elkton, Maryland

autumn growing colder,
respectability
loses its allure—
I dream of
being a pirate king

Perryville, Maryland

Slow Motion

a hundred years ago,
I would have run away
to sea, leaving
my debts, family, past,
for a new adventure

        Perryville, Maryland

"do what you love"
who then will pay me
to idle my days
in a wooden hull
on a lazy river?

        Perryville, Maryland

The Log of a Chesapeake Bay Skipjack

"Drudging Arsters": Seven Foot Knoll, off Baltimore

The skipjack Martha Lewis *is an oyster boat. That's what she was made to do, and that's what she keeps doing. It was a stipulation of her major donor at the time of her restoration that she be kept working as an oyster boat. Each year, in November, we move the boat to a marina near Sparrows Point. They let us stay free in exchange for us bringing them oysters. It's an equitable deal. We go out twice a week and take paying passengers who get to experience working aboard a skipjack and eating the freshest oysters they'll ever taste, straight out of the Bay.*

Yesterday we caught eight bushels. We lost one dredge overboard when it snapped its line—half an inch of steel cable parting with a sound like a rifle shot. Earlier in the week we had our first accidental overboard when a crew member was on the bowsprit to tie the jib and a gust of wind knocked her off. She was safely retrieved, but informed the crew that Captain Greg makes a quick pick up, the water is indeed 58 degrees, and the bottom of the boat is nice and clean.

This is our idea of 'fun'!

Slow Motion

<u>November 9, Friday</u>

a face full
of cold wind—
I man the helm
while the crew
hoist the sails

Patapsco River

only human—
forgetting to
untie the sails
before attempting
to raise the main

Patapsco River

oyster dredging—
a henley, a sweater,
a sweatshirt, a slicker,
a hat, a hood,
gloves inside of rubber gloves

Patapsco River

The Log of a Chesapeake Bay Skipjack

the naiveté of tourists—
the passenger asks if
he'll really need
his rubber boots
when we start dredging

Patapsco River

last to receive
my gear,
I wind up
with two left
rubber gloves

Seven Foot Knoll

oyster dredging—
hands cold inside
the rubber gloves

Seven Foot Knoll

Slow Motion

the roar
of the winder—
the captain
gives orders
by revving the engine

        Seven Foot Knoll

without words
the captain gives
two thumbs down—
both dredges
go over the sides

        Seven Foot Knoll

the squeal
of steel cable
over rollers,
the thrum
of the engine

        Seven Foot Knoll

The Log of a Chesapeake Bay Skipjack

the dredge thuds
onto the oysterboards;
soon oysters
are flying at me
to be cleaned and culled

Seven Foot Knoll

ninety seconds
per lick:
haul the dredge,
cull, clean,
drop the dredge again

Seven Foot Knoll

blue crabs
too small to keep
caught up
in the dredge

Seven Foot Knoll

Slow Motion

dark exhaust
from the winder engine,
columns of smoke
from the industries
on Sparrows Point

Seven Foot Knoll

a moment of nostalgia,
I recognize
a former captain's
handwriting
on the oysterboards

Seven Foot Knoll

suddenly,
a sound like a shot—
the cable parts
and the dredge
is lost on the bottom

Seven Foot Knoll

The Log of a Chesapeake Bay Skipjack

one dredge lost,
the other damaged,
a purple laundry jug
to mark the place
for salvage

      Seven Foot Knoll

dredging for
the lost dredge
with our
remaining dredge . . .
but no luck

      Seven Foot Knoll

work keeps me warm—
the chill of the lost dredge

      Seven Foot Knoll

Slow Motion

my aching legs
on my knees culling,
my aching hands
scraping mussels
from oysters

Seven Foot Knoll

warm enough
while working,
but cold on my
lunch break

Seven Foot Knoll

hot chocolate
hot off the stove,
I don't dawdle
but it's cold
before I finish

Seven Foot Knoll

The Log of a Chesapeake Bay Skipjack

culling the
broken shells,
small ones,
rocks, mud
with cold hands

    Seven Foot Knoll

eight bushels
with one dredge—
big ones
tender and salty
on a November day

    Seven Foot Knoll

a broken bushel
tears a hole in
my jeans,
but fortunately,
not in me

    Seven Foot Knoll

Slow Motion

two o'clock
in the afternoon—
already
the rosy hues
of winter sunset

Patapsco River

if I were
an osprey,
I would not mind
this winter cold,
working for my dinner

Patapsco River

jeans, jacket, hat,
all muddy after
a day of oystering

Patapsco River

The Log of a Chesapeake Bay Skipjack

with worn out
sailing gloves I pull
the torn leech,
me and the boat
both feeling our age

Patapsco River

woman overboard—
tying down the jib,
a gust of wind
on an otherwise
cold and calm day

Patapsco River

"Captain Zen"—
a crew member overboard
a lost dredge,
and not a word of profanity
from his lips

Patapsco River

Slow Motion

wet, muddy, cold, tired—
the skipjack safely
back in port

        North Point Cove

tying up the boat,
stowing gear,
one bushel to
the marina owner
pays the dockage

        North Point Cove

Epilogue: Someone Else's Adventure

Today the *Martha Lewis* took on a load of grapes from a local vineyard and transported them across the Chesapeake Bay to a winery while on her way to a skipjack race in Cambridge. I crewed the last time, so couldn't go on this trip. I helped load four thousand pounds of grapes into her hull and on the deck. Then I watched her sail away.

> watching the boat
> sail away without me,
> somebody else
> going to adventure
> this autumn morning

As she dwindled in the distance, I reminded the people on the dock, "Don't watch her out of sight. If you do, she won't come back." That's an old Irish superstition I learned from my mother.

The Log of a Chesapeake Bay Skipjack

Notes

15 In waterman's lingo, the crew 'carries' a boat to her destination, especially when she is laden with cargo.

16.2 Winder box: the wooden box that covers the engine that runs the winder (winch) to lift the dredges.

18.1 Black pennants: in the Upper Bay, crab-pots are marked with pennants or flags to make them more visible. In the lower bay, no such markers are used, and the pots are nearly invisible.

19.2 When 'mainsail' is pronounced properly, it only has one syllable.

21.3 Reef: folds of the sail tied to the boom to reduce the sail area. The amount of sail raised is matched to the amount of wind. *Martha* normally keeps one reef in at all times (she has four), but to prepare for the race we shook it out and attached the club to the head of the mainsail, thereby enabling us to raise every inch of canvas we have.

22.1 One span was built, then years later, the other span was built. They don't look anything alike from the water.

23.1 Tanbark: A natural preservative used in some old sails turns them a reddish brown.

23.3 Ego Alley: Otherwise known as Spa Creek, where people go to see and be seen in a conspicuous display of wealth.

24.1 Midis: Midshipmen from the U. S. Naval Academy. The female cadets are also midship*men*. The uniforms are identical.

26.1 Thomas Point Light: one of the seamarks of the Chesapeake Bay. Sometimes called a 'screwpile' because of its octagonal house with the light on top, but the term 'screwpile' actually refers to the method of securing the foundation to the shoals and not the house itself.

28.1 Sharp's Island Light was nudged into a lean by a heavy blow in 1970 and has remained that way ever since. It is located on what are now the Sharp Island Shoals, Sharp Island having completely eroded away. It is one of several vanishing islands in the Chesapeake, a natural process that has been going on for millennia, but which is getting worse with global warming.

28.2 Calvert Cliffs. One of the Seven Wonders of the Chesapeake Bay, these cliffs are the highest shoreline on the Chesapeake Bay. Rising hundreds of feet high in places, they go on for thirty miles. If they were white, they'd rival the Cliffs of Dover.

Slow Motion

28.3 Bell buoy: has a bell that is rung by the waves rocking it. It sounds like a church bell.

30.1 Topping lift: A line that runs from the aft end of the boom to the masthead. Leech: the back edge of the sail.

31.1 Lazyjacks: Lines rigged as a lattice to catch the sails when they drop to avoid burying the deck. With 1942 square feet of canvas, *Martha's* sails are several times larger than my apartment.

31.2 Halyards: The lines used to haul up the sails.

32.1 We listened to Radio Margaritaville all the way down. Then Deal Island had a Jimmy Buffet tribute band in concert—I have now fulfilled my lifetime quota of Jimmy Buffet and I don't have to listen to him ever again.

33 'Rafted' means tied up beside another vessel because there is no dock space. After the race, we wound up in the middle of a raft of six vessels. This means that the interior vessels must be walked across by the crews of the outer vessels, leading to a certain amount of camaraderie.

34.2 Miss Ida May is a grand old lady, and the skipjack *Ida May* is named after her. The skipjack being under repair, Miss Ida May came aboard the *Martha Lewis* for the race instead.

35.2 A sailboat cannot hold still on the water; it is always being pushed by the wind and tide. The boats parade up and down the starting line while waiting for the signal.

35.3 The *City of Crisfield*, under Captain Art, is one of the Deal Island skipjacks. Last year he suckered us. That was Captain Greg's first race. Reasoning that Captain Art knew the local waters better than he did, Captain Greg followed him. But the *City of Crisfield* has a little less draft than the *Martha Lewis,* so Captain Art deliberately ran into shoals. *Martha* grounded and the *City of Crisfield* sailed away and left us behind.

36.1 This year we didn't follow Art. We chose our own course, which happened to run through a minefield of crab-pots. Meanwhile, the *City of Crisfield* ran far out to gain the best point of sail. She came screaming in on a broad reach to race us for the second mark. It is illogical to a landlubber, but going out of your way to travel a longer distance can actually be much faster with a sailboat.

37.2 Wing and wing: With the jib swung out to one side and the mainsail on the other, like a gull spreading its wings. *City of Crisfield* has a light plastic club on her jib, so she was able to wing out in the light air, but *Martha* has her original wooden club which was too heavy to do the same.

The Log of a Chesapeake Bay Skipjack

38.3 Ketch: a kind of two-masted sailboat; a popular rig for pleasure boats.

39.1 Never have I seen the Milky Way so huge and brilliant as at Wingate. The bridge of the Milky Way ran from tree line to tree line in a tremendous arch of stars.

40.1 Wingate is located on the Honga River. When we visited with Captain Ozylee and his wife Naomi, he showed us pictures and explained how his father, Captain Jim, used to use a boathook to keep contact with a dredge cable at all time. By the feel of the vibrations in the cable, he could tell what kind of bottom he had and what kind of load in the dredges. This is a trick used by the Honga River dredge captains, for which reason they were known as the Honga River Boathook Dredgers.

40.2 We got invited to sleep on Ozylee and Omi's screened in front porch. The mosquito is the official bird of Wingate, so sleeping on the Captain's screen porch was a welcome alternative to sleeping on deck. They let us use their shower and towels, too.

42.1 Next morning we were up at dawn and across the street to the market to get breakfast and supplies. When we walked in, the woman behind the register knew exactly who we were. Later, when we came back to get the ice we'd forgotten it was about 7:15 am. She looked at us in disapproval and said, "You boys haven't left yet?" We encountered crabbers coming back for 'lunch' after having spent several hours working already. I guess we must have seemed like dawdlers to her.

42.3 I was baffled by the yellow haze. Later I would learn it was smog all the way from Baltimore.

44.1 The Ritz of Havre de Grace was a tiny eclectic cafe with crochet doilies, chessboards, Frank Sinatra on the stereo, and six tables crammed together. A Blondie is like a Dagwood, only different.

46.2 Steams: any vessel under power is described as 'steaming' even though the days of coal-fired steam engines are long gone.

47.2 Poole Island Light: the first of many lighthouses built in the early 1800s by John Donahoo. Lighthouse building is one of those acts of altruism which has no logical explanation except for a desire to help others.

48.2 Poole Island became the property of the Army, which used it for artillery practice. It is off limits to the public because it is full of unexploded ordinance. Before it was used for target practice it was famous for its many springs and pools and the quality of the peaches grown there.

Slow Motion

49.1 Stick a stick: *Martha* is pretty sophisticated for a skipjack. In the old days, you climbed into the pushboat with a jury can of fuel and filled her up. Now we have a fuel line that runs from the pushboat to a tank in the hull of the skipjack. To find out how much fuel is left, open the gas cap and stick a stick in it. If the stick comes up dry, you're out of fuel.

49.2 Turkey Point: a hundred foot high bluff hosts another Donahoo lighthouse. It can be seen up to thirteen miles away. It is also home to a Hawkwatch, being a jumping off point for migratory birds flying along the Chesapeake Bay.

52.1 *Mal de disembarkation*: the opposite of *mal de mer*, it is the sensation that the world is continuing to bob gently up and down in spite of being on solid ground.

56.3 The *Martha Lewis'* mast is too tall to fit under the railroad bridge over the Susquehanna River. To go upriver, we have to call Amtrak and they send a team of men to crack the welds and handcrank the turntable open—that's how old the bridge is. We sail through and they immediately crank it closed and weld the rails shut again. We don't go upstream very often.

59.3 Gunfire: No cause for alarm, just a little night practice at the police shooting range.

62.3 Fishing Battery Light: Yet another lighthouse constructed by the irrepressible John Donahoo. It was his last. This time he not only built a light, but an artificial island used for processing fish.

63.2 Deadrise: A low, engine-powered work boat that looks something like a pickup truck with its cab and long low bed. Used for crabbing.

63.3 Salt line: The Chesapeake Bay is the estuary of the Susquehanna River, so it has a gradation from fresh at the source to salt at the mouth. In dry years the reduction in fresh water permits salt water to inundate higher up the Bay. Because blue crabs like moderate salinity, when the Wye River and other southern locations become too salty for them, they migrate north. Naturally, the watermen follow them. In 2007 it was so dry and the salt line so far north, they were crabbing in the mouth of the North East River.

64.2 Spesutia Island is part of the Aberdeen Proving Ground, where they test ordinance and conduct other military research.

72.3 Knapp Narrows is the narrow body of water that separates Tilghman Island from the mainland. A drawbridge manned 24/7 raises and lowers for the water traffic.

The Log of a Chesapeake Bay Skipjack

73.1 Since Captain Greg wanted to dock with the port side along the dock, it required us to snag a piling and use it as a pivot to swing *Martha* around so that she wound up pointing back the way she came, her larboard along the dock instead of her starboard. Worked like a charm—the first time.

76.2 Starting about four-thirty in the morning, the deadrises (crab boats) come through real regular. The drawbridge makes an awful racket rising for them. You couldn't sleep late if you wanted to.

76.3 It's so darn early not even the birds are up.

77.2 Pound nets are used to trap fish. So called because fish are stupid enough they rarely find their way out of the 'pound' or corral at the end of the nets. This is very convenient for the birds.

77.3 Tilghman's Island, once a watermen's town and nothing more, is starting to suffer the same ridiculous development that plagues places closer to Baltimore and Washington, DC.

81.3 The James Islands, north of Taylor Island, not to be confused with Janes Island, on the Tangier Sound.

82.3 Shearwaters: a kind of bird. I have seen flocks in excess of a hundred swirling across the water just ahead of our bow.

84.1 Snagging a crab pot would mean getting it fouled in the propellor, which would be bad.

84.2 The captain's fianceé couldn't reach him on his cell phone, so she called somebody else, and that captain zipped over to deliver the message.

84.3 The captain of the deadrise is also the owner of *Martha's* sister boat, the *Lady Katie*. Last year when we broke half our mast hoops in a race, he gave us *Katie's* mast hoops to repair *Martha*.

85.1 The Calvert Cliffs: There's only one harbor in all that stretch. It's pretty enough in fair weather, but you don't want to be blown onto that lee shore in a gale.

85.2 We saw several frigates and tenders steaming north. On the way home we found two ships anchored off Annapolis.

86.3 Modern lighthouses aren't very poetic in appearance. They're metal scaffolding to support warning signs and lights.

Slow Motion

87.2 It is the most marvelous thing in the world to look to every horizon and see no sign of civilization. The emptiness is a vast richness the landlubber can never imagine.

88.1 Solomons Lump Light is a distinctive lighthouse. A keeper's house originally occupied the caisson with the tower making up a corner of the facility. When the light was automated and the house removed, the tower remained where it was, off-center.

90.3 An empty fuel tank is not a crisis. We simply switch fuel tanks. Besides, you're never truly stuck when you have sails.

92.3 The *Ruby* is a three-log sailing canoe built in 1895. The log sailing canoe is a vessel peculiar to the Chesapeake Bay. Early colonists found the Native American dugout to be too small for their needs, so they made larger dugouts by laying three, five, or seven logs side by side, then hollowing them out with axe and adze.

93.2 Red Cap Creek debouches into the Big Annemessex River.

100.1 The great amount of manpower needed to crew the hundreds of skipjacks in the oyster fleet meant that desegregation occurred on the water before it did on land. Cook was one of the first positions that opened to African American men. Other African Americans served as deckhands in mixed crews, and some were even able to buy their own skipjacks and go into business for themselves.

102.2 Our crew is scrupulous about sobriety while under way. After the boat is securely docked and the public has gone home do we indulge. All crew on the *Martha Lewis* are subject to Department of Transportation (DOT) drug and alcohol testing.

104.2 The weather radio warned of possible storms, but while we got some wind, the rain and storm never materialized.

106.2 Harbor cover: an awning spread over the deck from mast to stern. About four feet off the deck, it keeps the rain and dew off during the night. It holds a small amount of heat too. We sleep on deck—*Martha's* berths are rustic, to put it mildly.

108.3 Headboat: a boat that charges by the head to take sportsmen fishing. Many watermen who are unable to make a living fishing, crabbing, or oystering turn to chartering sport fishermen to try and keep their boats working on the water.

The Log of a Chesapeake Bay Skipjack

109.3 It once held a fish-processing factory. In the early 1900s Crisfield was a town of 28,000; today the population has fallen to less than a tenth of that as the Bay has ceased to yield its bounties.

112.2 The condos of Crisfield are mostly empty, but lit up at night to give the illusion of occupancy.

114.3 You can tell the temperature by the number of pleasure boats on the water. The warmer it is, the more of them there are.

117.1 Fine on: at an angle close to the bowsprit, as opposed to 'broad on' at an angle wide from the bowsprit.

118.2 This was the same maneuver we performed successfully on our way down. This time we had the wind and tide running strongly towards the drawbridge. I'd shaken out the line, but it fouled and dropped short.

119.2 Samson post: a very sturdy post in the bow of the boat to which the bowlines are tied. The usual docking procedure is to wrap the line around it several times and use it to control the boat.

120.2 The skipjack broke her nose on the bulwark protecting the bridge, swung broadside across the channel, and made some yacht owners very nervous. We got her under control and tried again. Once again the line fouled and dropped short, but a man on the dock grabbed it and put it around the piling.

120.3 I tried to get a turn around the samson post, but the wet rope kept sliding through my hands and *Martha* swung wide again. I got the rope tight on the post, but the rope pinched my glove and my hand was pinned to the post. I couldn't wrap any more turns around the post because doing so would have laid the rope over my hand itself. I yanked my hand as hard as I could to get it out of there.

122.1 All polydactyl cats are descended from a six-toed ship's cat that landed in the 1600s, or so I'm told.

122.3 We debated alternatives to the missing spatula, such as a scraper covered with tar, but opted to borrow a spatula from the restaurant instead.

123.2 Poplar Island must have received its name via the same logic that induces people to call a tall man 'Shorty' and a bald man 'Curly.'

124.1 The rest of the crew had pancakes, but I'm allergic to wheat. I had milk and Rice Krispies instead.

Slow Motion

124.3 The vehicles running over the Bay Bridge make the entire structure hum loudly. It's an otherworldly noise that people in their vehicles never hear.

126.1 Smogbank: Baltimore has bad smog. With the wind blowing out of the southwest that day, it laid a huge, ugly, low, brown cloud on the water all the way to the Eastern Shore. I used to wonder why living in a rural area as I do we would get ozone alerts—now I know. Baltimore's pollution reaches that far. (Ozone is the principal ingredient making up smog.)

127.1 Boom lift: line used to support the weight of the boom. It was badly frayed, so we spliced it. A marlinspike makes it easier to open the cuntlines when splicing. This perfectly respectable nautical term was adopted by landlubbers and turned into something else.

127.2 Range light: a marker on the Chesapeake Bay. They run north from Poole Island to the Elk River, showing freighters the way to the C & D Canal.

128.2 Smog and smoke are definitely different. Smoke rises in a column to a great height, eventually developing an anvil top like a thunderhead. Smog is heavier and lies on the ground in a smothering blanket. Forest fires smell better, too.

129.3 The Sand Islands are nothing but dredge spoil and have no official name. They're a favorite destination for boaters who fish, swim, build bonfires on the beaches, camp, and so forth. The 'Redneck Yacht Club' is a country song by Craig Morgan.

130.2 Hatem Bridge: The Route 40 bridge over the Susquehanna River, voted "Most Beautiful Bridge in America" when it was built in 1947.

140.2 Dredge: a large metal rake with a bag attached, dragged along the bottom to rake up oysters. A dredge weighs a hundred pounds empty.

141.2 Lick: a pass over the oysterbeds with the dredges down.

142.1 Winder engine: engine for the winch used to haul the dredges aboard; revving the engine is the signal to raise or lower the dredges.

142.2 Oysterboards: plywood laid on the deck and around the sides to protect the boat from the dredges.

143.1 Laundry jugs are used as cheap buoys by watermen. They are used to mark the location of lost gear for later retrieval.

144.1 The mussels attach themselves to the oysters, sometimes quite firmly, and must be knocked off.

The Log of a Chesapeake Bay Skipjack

144.3 All work is done on the open deck. Only the cook goes below to work in the tiny galley to make the oyster stew on the two burner stove. The weather was sufficiently cold on deck that by the time I had finished drinking my hot chocolate, it had gone cold.

147.2 I wasn't actually aboard when she went over, but I heard about it. She was safely retrieved, *Martha's* first accidental overboard since her restoration in the winter of 1993-1994.

148.2 The legal limit is 150 bushels a day. Our eight bushels sold for $50 a piece. The proceeds went to support the boat. *Martha Lewis* is owned by the non-profit Chesapeake Heritage Conservancy, so all the crew are volunteers except the captain, who is a licensed professional. However, had *Martha* been a for-profit boat, the take would have been divided as follows: $50 x 8 bushels = $400. 30% to the boat for maintenance = $120. Leaving $280 to be divided among the crew, typically 6 - 8 men = $40 each, for 7 hours labor, which is less than $6 a hour —which is why no one makes a living with a skipjack any more.

www.ingramcontent.com/pod-product-compliance
Lightning Source LLC
Chambersburg PA
CBHW071722090426
42738CB00009B/1845